PHONICS
CONNECTIONS

Plant Parts

by Wiley Blevins

capstone
classroom

A plant has many parts. Most plants have roots, a stem, and leaves. Flowers grow on some types of plants. Each part helps the plant live and grow. Look at this plant's parts.

The plant is held in the soil by its roots.
The roots take in water too.

We can eat the roots of some plants.
A carrot is the root of a carrot plant. When you munch on a carrot, you are eating the plant's root.

The stem helps hold up the plant. Leaves grow on the stem. Water moves up the stem to the leaves.

The trunk of a tree is a stem. Water moves up the tree trunk. The water goes to the leaves of the tree.

The leaves of a plant have a big job. They make food for the plant. The leaves use water, sunlight, and air to make food. Flowers bloom on many plants.

The flowers have small seeds in them. These seeds could be used to grow new plants.